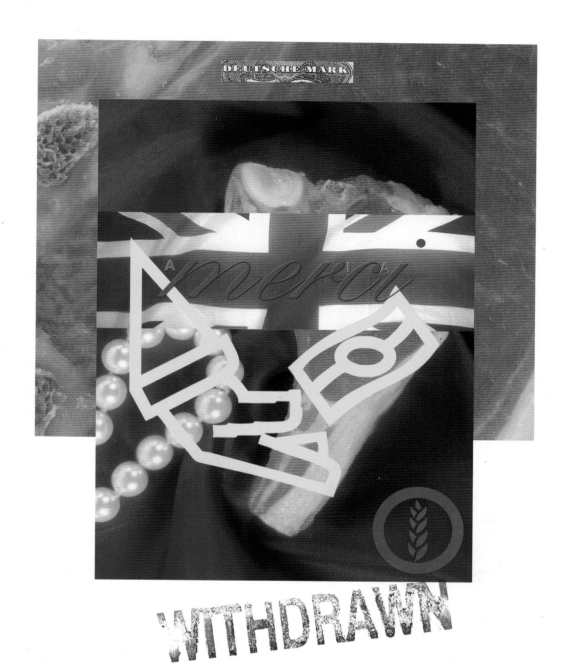

NillustrationW

BOOTH-CLIBBORN EDITIONS

Editeur EDITOR	EDWARD BOOTH-CLIBBORN
Mise en page BOOK DESIGN	JONATHAN BARNBROOK
Photographie [sauf photos de légumes] PHOTOGRAPHY [EXCEPT VEGETABLE PHOTOGRAPHY]	TOMOKO YONEDA
Photos De Légumes VEGETABLE PHOTOGRAPHY	DAVID GILL
Photos D'Archives STOCK PHOTOGRAPHY	THE IMAGE BANK
Police de caractères a barres macintosh fournie par MACINTOSH BARCODE FONT SUPPLIED BY	COMPUTALABEL
Traduction TRANSLATION	CATHERINE BALLADE
	FREDERIQUE GENAUX
	LINGUAFRANCA
	PAUL WILLIAMS
Conseils Techniques TECHNICAL SUPPORT	
Imprimé Par PRINTED BY	AMILCARE PIZZI, ITALIA

DISTRIBUTED IN THE UNITED
KINGDOM AND WORLD DIRECT MAIL:
INTERNOS BOOKS
18 COLVILLE ROAD
LONDON W3 8BL
UNITED KINGDOM

DISTRIBUTED IN FRANCE:
SOFEDIS
29 RUE SAINT SULPICE
PARIS 75006
FRANCE

BOOK TRADE FOR THE REST
OF THE WORLD:
HEARST BOOKS INTERNATIONAL
1350 AVENUE OF THE AMERICAS
NEW YORK NY 10019
USA

BOOTH-CLIBBORN EDITIONS
COPYRIGHT ©1992
ISBN 0 904866 97 1

Credits

II *Credits*
    CREDITS

III *Contents*
    TABLE DES MATIERES

IV *Foreword*
    AVANT-PROPOS

1   *Editorial*
    JOURNAUX, MAGAZINES

2   *Books*
    LIVRES

3   *Advertising*
    PUBLICITE

4   *Posters*
    AFFICHES

5   *Design*
    DESIGN

6   *Unpublished professional*
    PROFESSIONNELS NON PUBLIES

7   *Students*
    ETUDIANTS

8   *Index*
    INDEX

Sometime in 1993 *should see*
the opening of our new European Illustration Centre
in Hull, marked by an exhibition of original work culled from
past editions of 'European Illustration' and contemporary
contributions drawn from the present. □ The past will take us
back almost twenty years with paintings and drawings by
artists and illustrators whose work and reputation 'European
Illustration' has helped establish. □ The present
is to be found IN THIS NEW BOOK. THE EIGHTEENTH IN OUR

SERIES, NOW RE-TITLED 'ILLUSTRATION NOW'.

IT'S CERTAINLY ONE OF THE MOST INTERESTING WE'VE PUT TOGETHER. LIKE MANY OF

ITS PREDECESSORS, IT CONTAINS NEW IDEAS FROM NEW NAMES DESTINED

TO BECOME WELL KNOWN IN THE FUTURE. UNLIKE LAST YEAR'S IN PART-

ICULAR, WITH ITS PLETHORA OF WORK FROM THE COUNTRIES OF THE OLD

EASTERN BLOC, IT OFFERS A MUCH MORE BALANCED VIEW OF CONTEMPOR-

ARY ILLUSTRATION IN EUROPE.

London

Paris

New York

F O R E W O R D

THROUGH EXCEPTIONAL QUALITY OF THE WORK ON SHOW, IT ALSO

CONFIRMS MY BELIEF THAT GOOD IDEAS AND GOOD TECHNIQUE ARE STILL

TO BE FOUND IN EVERY CORNER OF THE CONTINENT. AGAINST A BACKDROP

OF CONTINUING CHANGE THROUGHOUT EUROPE, WITH ALL ITS POLITICAL

UPHEAVALS AND ECONOMIC UNCERTANTITIES, MY HOPE IS THAT NEXT

YEAR'S 'ILLUSTRATION NOW' WILL PROVIDE A CERTAIN FOCUS FOR ALL

OUR ARTISTS AND ILLUSTRATORS, AND A BENCH-MARK FOR EXCELLENCE

THROUGHOUT OUR COMMUNITY OF NATIONS.

L'année 1993 verra s'ouvrir à Hull le nouveau Centre européen de l'illustration. Cet évènement sera marqué par une exposition comportant à la fois des travaux originaux extraits d'éditions précédentes de 'European Illustration' et des contributions contemporaines d'actualité. § Nous ferons à cette occasion un bond en arrière de presque vingt ans, avec des peintures et des dessins provenant d'artistes et d'illustrateurs pour lesquels 'European Illustration' a joué un rôle majeur, dans l'assise de leur réputation et dans la dissémination de leurs oeuvres. § Les travaux contemporains se trouvent dans ce nouveau livre. § Le dix-huitième dans notre série qui porte désormais le nouveau titre de 'Illustration Now', il est certainement l'un des plus intéressants que nous ayons jamais publié.

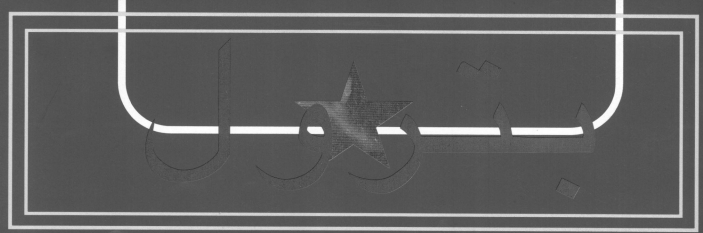

Propos

A l'image de beaucoup de ses prédécesseurs, il contient les idées nouvelles d'artistes destinés à une renommée future. § Contrairement à celui de l'an dernier, en particulier du fait de l'accumulation de travaux en provenance des pays de l'ancienne Europe de l'Est, ce volume présente une image plus équilibrée de l'illustration contemporaine en Europe. § De par la qualité exceptionnelle des travaux exposés, il ne fait que renforcer ma conviction que des idées et des techniques de qualité sont encore à découvrir aux quatre coins du continent. § Dans l'atmosphère actuelle de changement incessant en Europe, avec ses soulèvements politiques et ses incertitudes économiques, mon plus grand espoir serait que le numéro à venir de 'Illustration Now' fournisse un centre d'intérêt pour tous nos artistes et illustrateurs, tout en étant un témoin d'excellence au travers de notre communauté.

editorial

★ الحياة فن ★

WASHINGTON, D.C.

journaux magazines

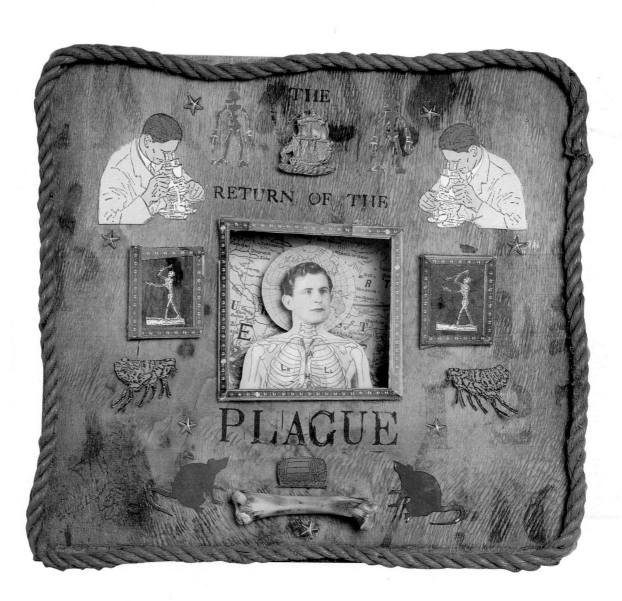

THE RETURN OF THE PLAGUE

LE RETOUR DE LA PESTE

THE RETURN OF THE PLAGUE   COVER ILLUSTRATION FOR GEOGRAPHICAL MAGAZINE

ILLUSTRATION DE

COUVERTURE POUR LE MAGAZINE GEOGRAPHICAL

DESIGNER   MAQUETTISTE
              SALLY DOUST
PUBLISHER   EDITEUR
       GEOGRAPHICAL MAGAZINE

MIXED MEDIA/MOYENS DIVERS

1.1

WALTER VAN LOTRINGEN

PETIT RESTAURANT

ILLUSTRATION FOR A SHORT STORY ABOUT A MAN REFLECTING ON HIS CHILDREN OUTGROWING HIM

ILLUSTRATION POUR UNE NOUVELLE SUR UN HOMME MEDITANT SUR LE FAIT QUE SES ENFANTS GRANDISSENT

DESIGNER MAQUETTISTE
ROON VAN SANTEN
PUBLISHER EDITEUR
HOLLAND HERALD MAGAZINE

MIXED MEDIA/MOYENS DIVERS

DESIGNER   MAQUETTISTE
          ROON VAN SANTEN
PUBLISHER   EDITEUR
          HOLLAND HERALD MAGAZINE

MIXED MEDIA/MOYENS DIVERS

WALTER VAN LOTRINGEN

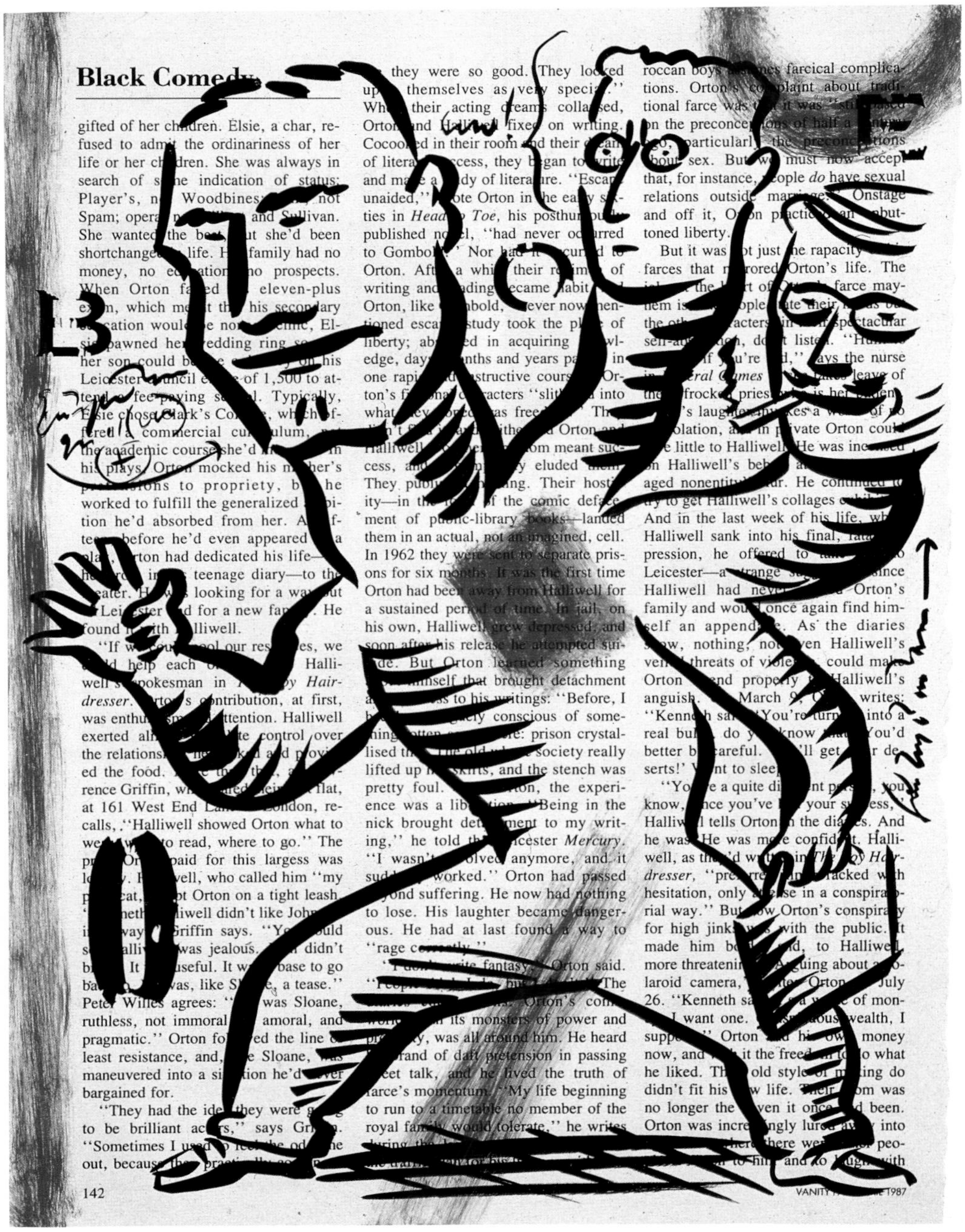

ILLUSTRATION FOR AN ARTICLE ON THE IDEAL MAN

BOEMAN

ILLUSTRATION POUR UN ARTICLE SUR L'HOMME IDEAL

PUBLISHER EDITEUR

PLAYBOY MAGAZINE

MIXED MEDIA/MOYENS DIVERS

+HE AGE WAVE ILLUS+RA+I⊕N F⊕R A FEA+URE ⊕N MARKE+ PR⊕SPEC+S ⊕VER +HE NEX+ HALF CEN+URY

LA VAGUE DE L'AGE ILLUS+RA+I⊕N P⊕UR UN AR+ICLE SUR LES PERSPEC+IVES C⊕MMERCIALES DE LA PREMIÈRE M⊕I+IE DU SIÈCLE PR⊕CHAIN

DESIGNER   MAQUE++IS+E
         GARY K⊕EPKE
PUBLISHER   EDI+EUR
    REDGA+E C⊕MMUNICA+I⊕NS

C⊕LLAGE, PEN, INK AND WA+ERC⊕L⊕UR/C⊕LLAGE, PLUME, ENCRE E+ AQUARELLE

I.5

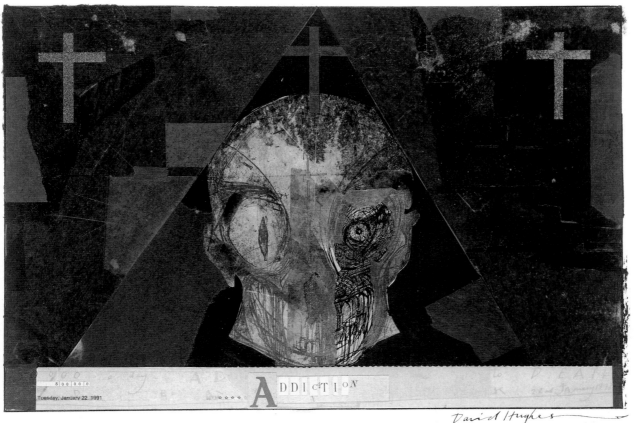

David Hughes

ADDIC+I⊕N ILLUS+RA+I⊕N F⊕R AN AR+ICLE ⊕N VARI⊕US F⊕RMS ⊕F ADDIC+I⊕N.

RANGING FR⊕M P⊕WER +⊕ ALC⊕H⊕L ADDIC+I⊕N

DÉPENDANCE ILLUS+RA+I⊕N P⊕UR UN AR+ICLE SUR

DIVERSES F⊕RMES DE DÉPENDANCES, ALLAN+ DE L'AM⊕UR DU P⊕UV⊕IR À L'ALC⊕⊕LISME

DESIGNER   MAQUE++IS+E
GRAHAM MI+CHENER
PUBLISHER   EDI+EUR
+HE ⊕BSERVER MAGAZINE

MIXED MEDIA/M⊕YENS DIVERS

DESIGNER   MAQUE++IS+E
GRAHAM MI+CHENER
PUBLISHER   EDI+EUR
+HE ⊕BSERVER MAGAZINE

MIXED MEDIA/M⊕YENS DIVERS

LEPROSY ILLUSTRATION FOR AN ARTICLE ON LEPROSY 'THE HEALING TOUCH'

LEPRE ILLUSTRATION POUR UN ARTICLE SUR LA LEEPRE INTITULE 'LE TOUCHER GUERISSEUR'

DAVID HUGHES

DESIGNER   MAQUETTISTE

GRAHAM MITCHENER

PUBLISHER   EDITEUR

THE OBSERVER MAGAZINE

MIXED MEDIA/MOYENS DIVERS

1.8

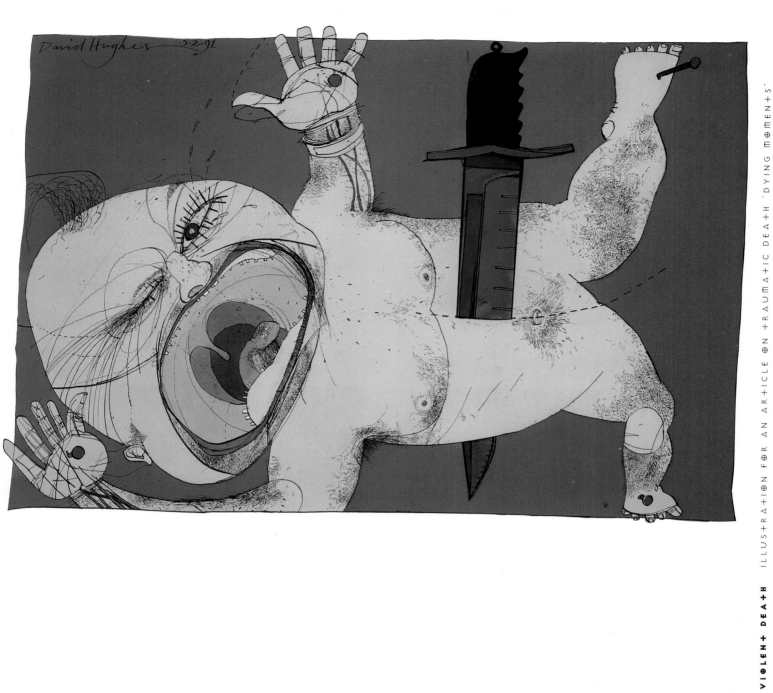

VI❶LEN+ DEA+H ILLUS+RA+I❶N F❶R AN AR+ICLE ❶N +RAUMA+IC DEA+H 'DYING M❶MEN+S'

M❶R+ VI❶LEN+E ILLUS+RA+I❶N P❶UR UN AR+ICLE SUR LES M❶R+S +RAUMA+ISAN+ES IN+I+ULE 'DERNIERS INS+AN+S'

DAVID HUGHES

DESIGNER   MAQUE++IS+E
GRAHAM MI+CHENER
PUBLISHER   EDI+EUR
+HE ❶BSERVER MAGAZINE

INK AND WA+ERC❶L❶UR/ENCRE E+ AQUARELLE

1.9

BRAD HOLLAND

DESIGNER   MAQUE++IS+E
HANS-GE⊕RG P⊕SPISCHIL
PUBLISHER   EDI+EUR
FRANKFUR+ER ALLGEMEINE ZEI+UNG

ACRYLIC/ACRYLIQUE

ILLUSTRATION TIREE D'UNE SERIE DE QUATRE POUR UN ARTICLE INTITULE 'DAS SPIEL DER MACHT'

BRAD HOLLAND

DESIGNER   MAQUETTISTE
HANS-GEORG POSPISCHIL
PUBLISHER   EDITEUR
FRANKFURTER ALLGEMEINE ZEITUNG

MIXED MEDIA/MOYENS DIVERS

I.11

SUBWAYS

DESIGNER   MAQUETTISTE
HANS-GEORG POSPISCHIL
PUBLISHER   EDITEUR
FRANKFURTER ALLGEMEINE ZEITUNG

ACRYLIC/ACRYLIQUE

ILLUSTRATION FOR FRANKFURTER ALLGEMEINE MAGAZIN

SUBWAYS

ILLUSTRATION POUR LE FRANKFURTER ALLGEMEINE MAGAZIN

BRAD HOLLAND

DESIGNER   MAQUETTISTE
HANS-GEORG POSPISCHIL
PUBLISHER   EDITEUR
FRANKFURTER ALLGEMEINE ZEITUNG

ACRYLIC/ACRYLIQUE

PUBLISHER   EDI+EUR
NEW SCIEN+IS+

MIXED MEDIA/M⊕YENS DIVERS

1.14

FR⊕M AN AR+ICLE IN +HE INDEPENDEN+ ⊕N SUNDAY '+HE AR+IS+IC P⊕LICIES ⊕F NICH⊕LAS SN⊕WMAN'

+IRE D'UN AR+ICLE DE L'INDEPENDAN+ ⊕N SUNDAY IN+I+ULE

'LES P⊕LI+IQUES AR+IS+IQUES DE NICH⊕LAS SN⊕WMAN'

DESIGNER   MAQUE++IS+E
              J⊕ DALE
PUBLISHER   EDI+EUR
    +HE INDEPENDEN+ ⊕N SUNDAY

WA+ERC⊕L⊕UR AND PAS+EL/AQUARELLE E+ PAS+EL

DANIEL PUDLES

ILLUSTRATION FOR AN ARTICLE ON WINE

ILLUSTRATION POUR UN ARTICLE SUR LE VIN

DESIGNER MAQUETTISTE
NEAL WATKINSON
PUBLISHER EDITEUR
THE OBSERVER MAGAZINE

WOODCUT AND COLLAGE/GRAVURE SUR BOIS ET COLLAGE

ILLUS+RA+I0N F0R AN AR+ICLE

'UN SCHEMA DIREC+EUR P0UR L'INF0RMA+IQUE'

ILLUS+RA+I0N P0UR UN AR+ICLE IN+I+ULE

DESIGNER   MAQUE++IS+E
              BENEDIC+E GENE+
PUBLISHER   EDI+EUR
        LE J0URNAL DU C.N.R.S.

MIXED MEDIA/M0YENS DIVERS

JEAN-CHRISTIAN KNAFF

PUBLISHER   EDITEUR
L'EVENEMENT DU JEUDI

WATERCOLOUR/AQUARELLE

JEALOUS GUY

ILLUSTRATION TIREE D'UNE SERIE DE QUATRE SUR LES CHANSONS DE JOHN LENNON

ONE OF A SERIES OF FOUR

ILLUSTRATIONS OF JOHN LENNON SONGS

PUBLISHER   EDITEUR
L'EVENEMENT DU JEUDI

ANDREJ DUDZINSKI

ONE OF A SERIES OF FOUR ILLUSTRATIONS OF JOHN LENNON SONGS

STRAWBERRY FIELDS FOREVER

ILLUSTRATION TIREE D'UNE SERIE DE QUATRE SUR LES CHANSONS DE JOHN LENNON

BENOIT JACQUES

PUBLISHER   EDITEUR
L'EVENEMENT DU JEUDI

WATERCOLOUR/AQUARELLE

ONE OF A SERIES OF FOUR ILLUSTRATIONS OF JOHN LENNON SONGS

I AM THE WALRUS

ILLUSTRATION THREE

D'UNE SERIE DE QUATRE SUR LES CHANSONS DE

JOHN LENNON

FIONA SMYTH

PUBLISHER EDITEUR

L'EVENEMENT DU JEUDI

WATERCOLOUR/AQUARELLE

ILLUS+RA+I⊕N P⊕UR UN AR+ICLE

ILLUS+RA+I⊕N F⊕R AN AR+ICLE 'P⊕WERS ⊕F +HE FRENCH PRESIDEN+'

ILLUS+RA+I⊕N IN+I+ULE 'LES P⊕UV⊕IRS DU PRÉSIDEN+ FRANÇAIS'

DESIGNER   MAQUE++IS+E
JIM McCLURE
PUBLISHER   EDI+EUR
BUSINESS MAGAZINE

PEN, INK AND WA+ERC⊕L⊕UR/PLUME, ENCRE E+ AQUARELLE

ILLUSTRATION FOR AN ARTICLE ON WOMEN AND AIDS

ILLUSTRATION POUR UN ARTICLE SUR LES FEMMES ET LE SIDA

ANNA OSTROWSKA

DESIGNER   MAQUETTISTE
              JAN FLIER
PUBLISHER   EDITEUR
UITGEVERSMAATSCHAPPIJ 'BONAVENTURA'

COLLAGE, ACRYLIC/COLLAGE, ACRYLIQUE

CAROLYN GOWDY

DESIGNER   MAQUETTISTE
NOEL CLARO
PUBLISHER   EDITEUR
VOGUE MAGAZINE

MIXED MEDIA/MOYENS DIVERS

ILLUS+RA+I⊕N F⊕R AN AR+ICLE '+⊕ GIVE ⊕NE'S +IME'

ILLUS+RA+I⊕N P⊕UR UN AR+ICLE IN+I+ULE 'D⊕NNER S⊕N +EMPS'

DESIGNER   MAQUE++IS+E
            CHRIS+IAN GAMBY
PUBLISHER   EDI+EUR
            C⊕SM⊕P⊕LI+AN

MIXED MEDIA/M⊕YENS DIVERS

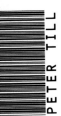

DESIGNER   MAQUETTISTE
RICHARD KRZYZAK
PUBLISHER   EDITEUR
NATIONAL MAGAZINE CO. LTD

PEN. INK. PENCIL AND WATERCOLOUR/PLUME. ENCRE. CRAYON ET AQUARELLE

DESIGNER   MAQUE++IS+E
RICHARD KRZYZAK
PUBLISHER   EDI+EUR
NA+I●NAL MAGAZINE C●. L+D

PEN, INK, PENCIL AND WA+ERC●L●UR/PLUME, ENCRE, CRAY●N E+ AQUARELLE

ILLUS+RA+I⊕N F⊕R AN AR+ICLE 'END ⊕F +HE PEER SH⊕W'

ILLUS+RA+I⊕N P⊕UR UN AR+ICLE IN+I+ULE

'FIN DU SPEC+ACLE'

DESIGNER   MAQUE++IS+E

CHRIS J⊕NES

PUBLISHER   EDI+EUR

IPC

PENCIL AND WA+ERC⊕L⊕UR/CRAY⊕N E+ AQUARELLE

DESIGNER   MAQUE++IS+E
S+EPHANIE PHELAN
PUBLISHER   EDI+EUR
INK MAGAZINES

PENCIL AND WA+ERC⊕L⊕UR/CRAY⊕N E+ AQUARELLE

COVER ILLUS+RA+I⊕N F⊕R C�⊕URRIER IN+ERNA+I⊕NAL. IN+R⊕DUCING AN AR+ICLE

'LES C⊕UACS DE LA N⊕UVELLE ALLEMAGNE'.

ILLUS+RA+I⊕N DE C⊕UVER+URE P⊕UR LE C⊕URRIER

IN+ERNA+I⊕NAL. PRÉSEN+AN+ UN AR+ICLE IN+I+ULE

PUBLISHER   EDI+EUR
C⊕URRIER IN+ERNA+I⊕NAL

⊕IL PAIN+ ⊕N PAPER/PEIN+URE À L'HUILE SUR PAPIER

STANISLAS BOUVIER

ILLUS+RA+I⊕N F⊕R AN AR+ICLE

'L'ARGEN+ NE FAI+ PAS LE B⊕NHEUR, MAIS JE PREFERE EN AV⊕IR PLU+⊕+ QUE L'INVERSE SIMPLEMEN+ P⊕UR DES RAIS⊕NS FINANCIERES'

ILLUS+RA+I⊕N P⊕UR UN AR+ICLE IN+I+ULE

STANISLAS BOUVIER

PUBLISHER   EDI+EUR
MAGAZINE VIVA

⊕IL PAIN+ ⊕N PAPER /PEIN+URE A L'HUILE SUR PAPIER

COVER ILLUSTRATION FOR COURRIER INTERNATIONAL. INTRODUCING AN ARTICLE

ILLUSTRATION DE COUVERTURE POUR LE COURRIER INTERNATIONAL. PRESENTANT UN ARTICLE INTITULE

'EUROPE, ETATS-UNIS: LES NOUVEAUX IMMIGRANTS'

PUBLISHER   EDITEUR
COURRIER INTERNATIONAL

OIL PAINT ON PAPER/PEINTURE A L'HUILE SUR PAPIER

STANISLAS BOUVIER

I.32

PETER SUTTON

ART EDITOR   EDITEUR ARTISTIQUE
          CAROLINE JEFFORD
DESIGNER   MAQUETTISTE
          LUCY HOLLOWAY
PUBLISHER   EDITEUR
          NURSING TIMES

ACRYLIC/ARCYLIQUE

1.33

ILLUS+RA+I⊕N P⊕UR LE RÉCI+ D'UN CRIME IN+I+ULÉ

ILLUS+RA+I⊕N F⊕R A CRIⅢE S+⊕RY

'IAL⊕SY'

PUBLISHER   EDI+EUR
A-ⅢAGASINE+, AF+ENP⊕S+EN

INK AND C⊕L⊕UR PENCIL/ENCRE E+ CRAY⊕N DE C⊕ULEUR

ILLUS+RA+I⊕N F⊕R AN AR+ICLE

ILLUS+RA+I⊕N P⊕UR UN AR+ICLE IN+I+ULE

'RESUME LIARS'

AB⊕U+ J⊕B CANDIDA+ES' EC⊕N⊕MY WI+H +HE +RU+H

SUR LA FAÇ⊕N D⊕N+ LES CANDIDA+S A UN EMPL⊕I EC⊕N⊕MISEN+ LA VERI+E

PHILIPPE LARDY

DESIGNER   MAQUE++IS+E
        PAMELA BERRY
PUBLISHER   EDI+EUR
        SAVVY MAGAZINE

⊕IL PAIN+ AND INK/PEIN+URE A L'HUILE E+ ENCRE

ART DIRECTOR   DIRECTEUR ARTISTIQUE
HANS-GEORG POSPISCHIL
PUBLISHER   EDITEUR
FRANKFURTER ALLGEMEINE MAGAZIN

OIL ON CANVAS/HUILE SUR TOILE

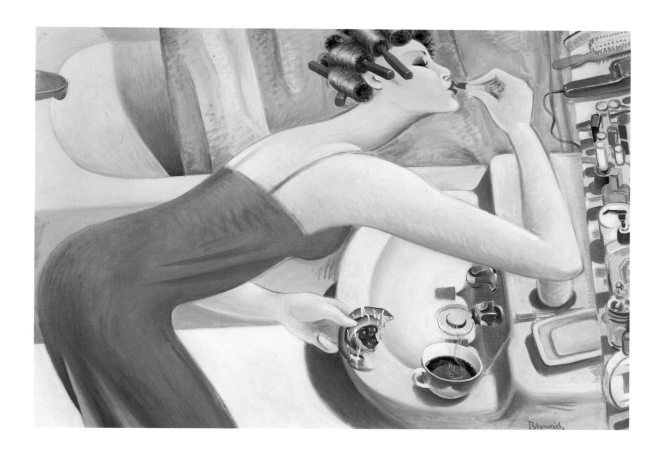

BREAKFAS+ IV [CAREER GIRL] ⊕NE ⊕F A SERIES ⊕F F⊕UR ILLUS+RA+I⊕NS F⊕R AN AR+ICLE 'DAS FRUHS+UCK'

PE+I+ DEJEUNER IV [FEMME PR⊕FESSI⊕NNELLE] ILLUS+RA+I⊕N +IREE D'UNE SERIE DE QUA+RE P⊕UR UN AR+ICLE IN+I+ULE 'DAS FRUHS+UCK'.

CHRISTOPH BLUMRICH

AR+ DIREC+⊕R   DIREC+EUR AR+IS+IQUE
HANS-GE⊕RG P⊕SPISCHIL
PUBLISHER   EDI+EUR
FRANKFUR+ER ALLGEMEINE MAGAZIN

⊕IL ⊕N CANVAS / HUILE SUR +⊕ILE

I.37

CYPRIAN

ILLUS+RA+I⊕N F⊕R AN AR+ICLE EXAMINING HIS+⊕RICAL +IES AND RELA+I⊕NSHIPS WI+HIN EUR⊕PE

DE ⊕N+V⊕ERING VAN EUR⊕PA ANN⊕ 1990 [L'ENLEVEMEN+ DE L'EUR⊕PE 1990 AP I-C]

ILLUS+RA+I⊕N P⊕UR UN AR+ICLE EXAMINAN+ LES LIENS E+ RELA+I⊕NS HIS+⊕RIQUES EN EUR⊕PE

DESIGNER   MAQUE++IS+E
KARIN MA+HIJSEN GERS+
PUBLISHER   EDI+EUR
DAGBLADUNIE/NRC - HANDELSBLAD

WA+ERC⊕L⊕UR/AQUARELLE

ILLUS+RA+I⊕N F⊕R AN AR+ICLE EXAMINING +HE BAD HABI+S ⊕F +HE DU+CH

ILLUS+RA+I⊕N P⊕UR UN AR+ICLE EXAMINAN+ LES MAUVAISES HABI+UDES DES H⊕LLANDAIS

DESIGNER   MAQUE++IS+E
L⊕UIS V⊕⊕G+
PUBLISHER   EDI+EUR
GEILLUS+RIEERDE PERS BV AVENUE

WA+ERC⊕L⊕UR/AQUARELLE

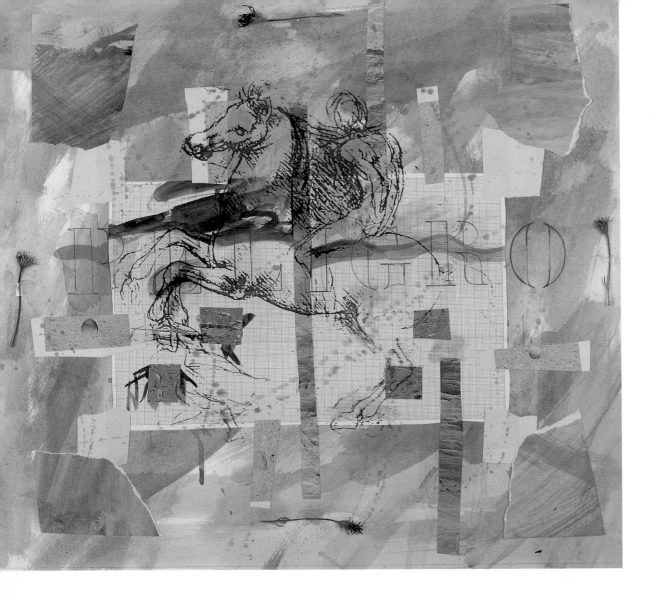

FOR AN ARTICLE ABOUT MAN'S INFLUENCE, BOTH DESTRUCTIVE AND BENEFICIAL, UPON THE ENVIRONMENT

POUR UN ARTICLE SUR L'INFLUENCE, TANT DESTRUCTRICE QUE SALUTAIRE, DE L'HOMME SUR SON ENVIRONNEMENT

PHILIP STANTON

DESIGNER   MAQUETTISTE
            FERRAN GRAU
ART DIRECTORS   DIRECTEURS ARTISTIQUES
    CARLOS PEREZ DE ROZAS & ROSA MUNDET
PUBLISHER   EDITEUR
        LA VANGUARDIA

COLLAGE. WATERCOLOUR/COLLAGE. AQUARELLE

COVER ILLUSTRATION FOR AN ARTICLE ABOUT THE PERSEVERING INFLUENCE OF MYTHS ON CONTEMPORARY SOCIETY

ILLUSTRATION DE COUVERTURE POUR UN ARTICLE SUR L'INFLUENCE PERSISTANTE

DES MYTHES SUR LA SOCIÉTÉ CONTEMPORAINE

PHILIP STANTON

DESIGNER   MAQUETTISTE
FERRAN GRAU
ART DIRECTORS   DIRECTEURS ARTISTIQUES
CARLOS PEREZ DE ROZAS & ROSA MUNDET
PUBLISHER   EDITEUR
LA VANGUARDIA

COLLAGE, ACRYLIC/COLLAGE, ACRYLIQUE

A DOUBLE-PAGE FROM A HANDBOUND BOOK OF PAINTINGS ON THE THEME OF LOVE

PAGE DOUBLE D'UN LIVRE DE PEINTURES, RELIÉ A LA MAIN, SUR LE THEME DE L'AMOUR

JAIME. 34 AÑOS. PLAYA BARCELONA

PHILIP STANTON

DESIGNER   MAQUETTISTE
JORDI OLMOS
PUBLISHER   EDITEUR
MEDIOS URBANOS EDITORA S.A.

ACRYLIC. OIL ON CANVAS/ACRYLIQUE. HUILE SUR TOILE

PAR+ ⊕F A PAIN+ING ILLUS+RA+ING BARCEL⊕NA FR⊕M I+S HIGHES+ P⊕IN+ +⊕ +HE SEA

DE+AIL D'UNE PEIN+URE REPRESEN+AN+ BARCEL⊕NE VUE DE S⊕N P⊕IN+ LE PLUS ELEVE JUSQU'A LA MER

DESIGNER   MAQUE++IS+E
J⊕RDI ⊕LM⊕S
PUBLISHER   EDI+EUR
MEDI⊕S URBAN⊕S EDI+⊕RA S.A.

MIXED MEDIA ⊕N PAPER/M⊕YENS DIVERS SUR PAPIER

1.43

FOR AN ARTICLE ABOUT LATIN AMERICA'S CONTROVERSIAL INHERITANCE OF THE SPANISH CONQUEST
POUR UN ARTICLE SUR L'HERITAGE CONTROVERSE DE LA CONQUETE ESPAGNOLE EN AMERIQUE LATINE

PHILIP STANTON

DESIGNER   MAQUETTISTE
                    FERRAN GRAU
ART DIRECTORS   DIRECTEURS ARTISTIQUES
        CARLOS PEREZ DE ROZAS & ROZA MUNDET
PUBLISHER   EDITEUR
            LA VANGUARDIA

COLLAGE

ILLUS+RA+I⊕N F⊕R AN AR+ICLE AB⊕U+ +AS+E

ILLUS+RA+I⊕N P⊕UR UN AR+ICLE SUR LE G⊕U+

PHILIP STANTON

DESIGNER   MAQUE++IS+E
                 FERRAN GRAU
AR+ DIREC+⊕RS   DIREC+EURS AR+IS+IQUES
    CARL⊕S PEREZ DE R⊕ZAS & R⊕ZA MUNDE+
PUBLISHER   EDI+EUR
           LA VANGUARDIA

ACRYLIC, PAS+EL/ACRYLIQUE, PAS+EL

PART OF A SERIES SHOWING DIFFERENT ASPECTS OF BARCELONA DURING THE EARLY HOURS

6:17 AM PANADERIA BALMES

TIRE D'UNE SERIE MONTRANT DIVERS ASPECTS DE BARCELONE AU PETIT MATIN

DESIGNER   MAQUETTISTE
                JORDI OLMOS
PUBLISHER   EDITEUR
    MEDIOS URBANOS EDITORA S.A.

ACRYLIC, PENCIL, GOUACHE/ACRYLIQUE, CRAYON, GOUACHE

PHILIP STANTON

CALENDRIER EN FORME DE TRYPTIQUE EXPRIMANT VISUELLEMENT LES EVENEMENTS DE L'ANNEE A VENIR A BARCELONE

CALENDAR TRYPTICH VISUALLY EXPRESSING THE EVENTS OF THE COMING YEAR IN BARCELONA

DESIGNER   MAQUETTISTE
JORDI OLMOS
PUBLISHER   EDITEUR
MEDIOS URBANOS EDITORA S.A.

ACRYLIC, OIL ON CANVAS/ACRYLIQUE, HUILE SUR TOILE

ILLUSTRATION FOR AN ARTICLE ABOUT HUSBANDS WHO SEND THEIR WIVES AWAY TO MENTAL HOSPITALS

ILLUSTRATION POUR UN ARTICLE SUR LES MARIS QUI ENVOIENT LEUR FEMME EN HOPITAL PSYCHIATRIQUE

DESIGNER   MAQUETTISTE
JUDITH M. OSTERWALDER
PUBLISHER   EDITEUR
MARIE FRANCE

SCRATCHBOARD AND INK/CARTE A GRATTER ET ENCRE

STUART BRIERS

DESIGNER   MAQUETTISTE
        LUCY PIDDUCK
PUBLISHER   EDITEUR
      EUROBUSINESS LTD

ACRYLIC/ACRYLIQUE

ILLUSTRATION FOR AN ARTICLE ON MUGGING IN NEW YORK

'BONFIRE OF THE SANITIES'

ILLUSTRATION POUR UN ARTICLE SUR LES AGRESSIONS A NEW YORK INTITULE

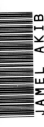

DESIGNER   MAQUETTISTE
       GRAHAM MITCHENER
PUBLISHER   EDITEUR
    THE OBSERVER MAGAZINE

CHALK AND PASTEL/CRAIE ET AQUARELLE

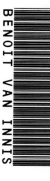

BART VAN LEEUWEN

DE WAAKHONDEN

ART DIRECTOR   DIRECTEUR ARTISTIQUE
JANNEKE NIEZEN AND SABINE
PUBLISHER   EDITEUR
QUOTE BV

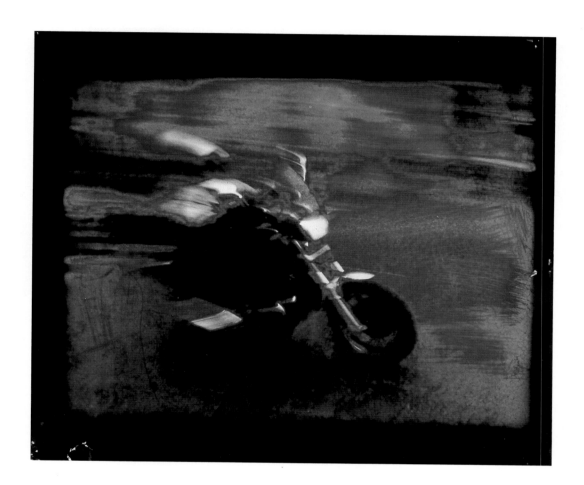

SAGI++ARIUS

SAGI++AIRE

JEAN-LUC DE ZORZI

DESIGNER   MAQUE++IS+E
            ARIANE BONDOI+
PUBLISHER   EDI+EUR
            MAX

MIXED MEDIA/MOYENS DIVERS

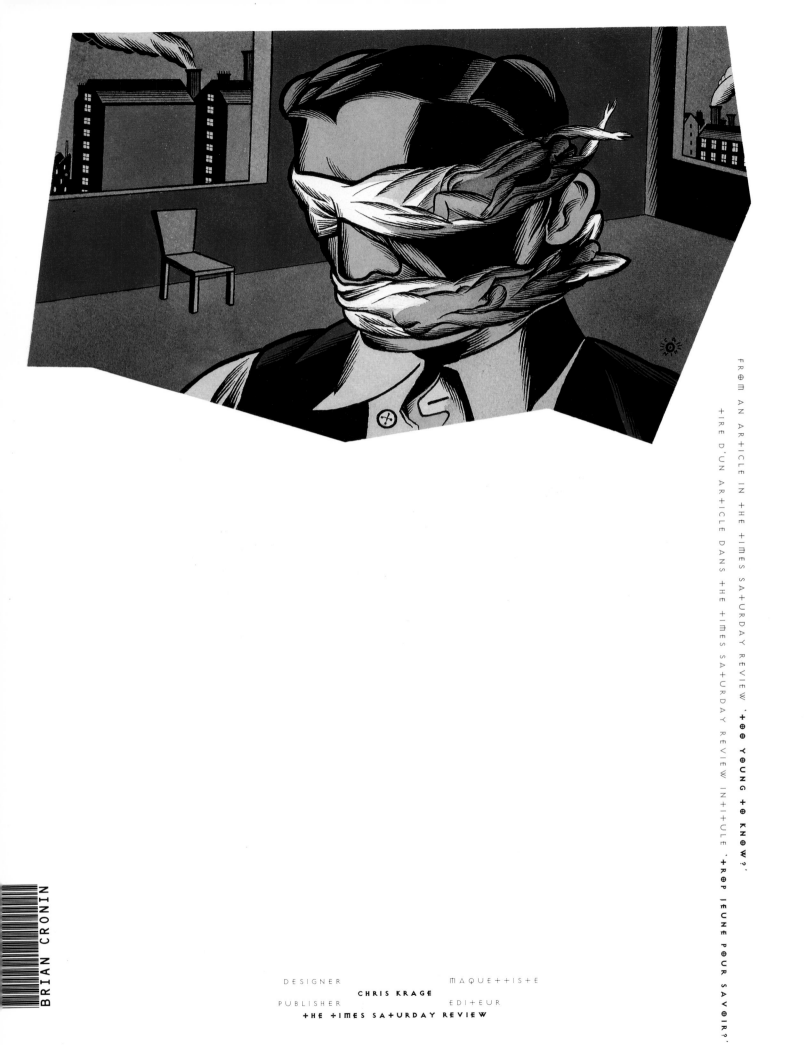

FR⊕M AN AR+ICLE IN +HE +IMES SA+URDAY REVIEW '+⊕⊕ Y⊕UNG +⊕ KN⊕W?'.

+IRE D'UN AR+ICLE DANS +HE +IMES SA+URDAY REVIEW IN+I+ULE '+R⊕P JEUNE P⊕UR SAV⊕IR?'.

DESIGNER MAQUE++IS+E
CHRIS KRAGE
PUBLISHER EDI+EUR
+HE +IMES SA+URDAY REVIEW

PEN, INK AND WA+ERC⊕L⊕UR/PLUME, ENCRE E+ AQUARELLE

FROM AN ARTICLE IN THE TIMES SATURDAY REVIEW 'SMILE PLEASE, YOU'RE UNDER ARREST'.

TIRE D'UN ARTICLE DANS THE TIMES SATURDAY REVIEW INTITULE 'SOURIEZ S'IL VOUS PLAIT,

VOUS ETES EN ETAT D'ARRESTATION'.

DESIGNER   MAQUETTISTE

CHRIS KRAGE

PUBLISHER   EDITEUR

THE TIMES SATURDAY REVIEW

PEN. INK. WATERCOLOUR AND ACRYLIC/PLUME. ENCRE. AQUARELLE ET ACRYLIQUE

FR⊕M AN AR+ICLE IN +HE +IMES SA+URDAY REVIEW 'AN AFFAIR ⊕F +HE MIND'

RELA+ING FRANCE'S C⊕⊕LING RELA+I⊕NSHIP WI+H I+S IN+ELLEC+UALS

+IRE D'UN AR+ICLE DANS +HE +IMES SA+URDAY REVIEW IN+I+ULE 'UNE AFFAIRE D'ESPRI+'

EXP⊕SAN+ LE REFR⊕IDISSEMEN+ DES RELA+I⊕NS EN+RE FRANCE E+ SES IN+ELLEC+UELS

DESIGNER   MAQUE++IS+E
          CHRIS KRAGE
PUBLISHER   EDI+EUR
+HE +IMES SA+URDAY REVIEW

PEN, INK AND WA+ERC⊕L⊕UR/CRAY⊕N, ENCRE E+ AQUARELLE

DESIGNER   MAQUETTISTE
YVES-MARIE MAQUET
PUBLISHER   EDITEUR
IMPRIMERIE NATIONALE

INK, COLOUR PENCIL AND WATERCOLOUR/ENCRE, CRAYON DE COULEUR ET AQUARELLE

2.1

COVER FOR AN ANTHOLOGY, LARGELY COMPRISING THE WORK OF LATIN AMERICAN WRITERS

SOHO SQUARE III

COUVERTURE D'UNE ANTHOLOGIE,

COMPRENANT PRINCIPALEMENT DES ŒUVRES D'ECRIVAINS LATINO-AMERICAINS

JEFF FISHER

PUBLISHER   EDITEUR

BLOOMSBURY

ACRYLIC/ACRYLIQUE

2.2

CHANGE FOR VIRGINIA WOOLF'S BIOGRAPHY OF ROGER FRY

COUVERTURE DE LA BIOGRAPHIE DE VIRGINIA WOOLF PAR ROGER FRY

JEFF FISHER

PUBLISHER   EDITEUR
HOGARTH PRESS

ACRYLIC/ACRYLIQUE

2.3

ILLUS+RA+I⊕N F⊕R GABRIEL GARCIA MARQUEZ'S '1⊕⊕ YEARS ⊕F S⊕LI+UDE'

ILLUS+RA+I⊕N P⊕UR '1⊕⊕ ANS DE S⊕LI+UDE' DE GABRIEL GARCIA MARQUEZ

DESIGNERS   M A Q U E + I S + E S
ANDERS LINDH⊕LM, GE⊕RGE SHARP
PUBLISHER   EDI+EUR
PAN B⊕⊕KS

G⊕UACHE + WA+ERC⊕L⊕UR/G⊕UACHE + AQUARELLE

LARA 7/6 1990

LARA HARWOOD

DESIGNER   MAQUETTISTE
        JANE BROMHAM
PUBLISHER   EDITEUR
        HARPER COLLINS

COLLAGE + WATERCOLOUR/COLLAGE + AQUARELLE

COVER FOR A BOOK, 'CREATIVE ASTROLOGY', ON THE EXPERIENTIAL UNDERSTANDING OF THE HOROSCOPE

COUVERTURE POUR UN LIVRE INTITULE 'L'ASTROLOGIE CREATIVE', SUR LA COMPREHENSION EMPIRIQUE DE L'HOROSCOPE

LIZ PYLE

DESIGNER   MAQUETTISTE
VAL PIGEON
PUBLISHER   EDITEUR
THE AQUARIAN PRESS

PASTEL ON PAPER/PASTEL SUR PAPIER

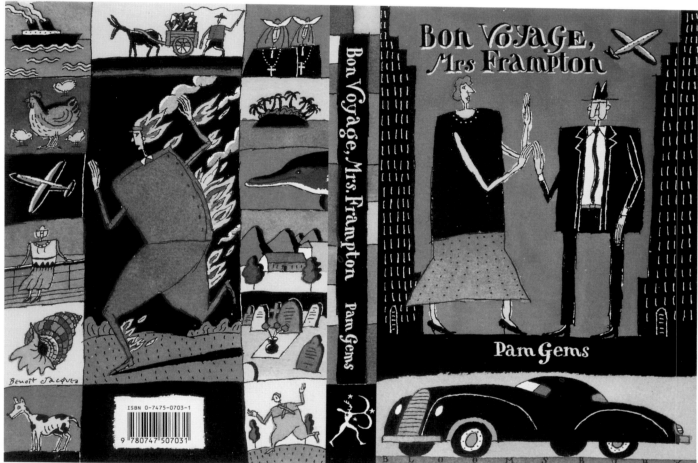

PUBLISHER   EDITEUR

BLOOMSBURY

BENOIT JACQUES

PEN, INK AND WATERCOLOUR/PLUME, ENCRE ET AQUARELLE

FACADE ILLUSTRATION FOR A BOOK 'SANDMAN: DREAM COUNTRY', DEPICTING A LONELY, IMMORTAL WOMAN, SURROUNDED BY MASKS OF HERSELF, WISHING TO DIE

FACADE ILLUSTRATION POUR UN LIVRE INTITULE 'MARCHAND DE SABLE: PAYS DES REVES', DECRIVANT UNE FEMME SEULE ET IMMORTELLE ENTOUREE DE MASQUES LA REPRESENTANT ET QUI VEUT MOURIR

DAVE MC KEAN

PUBLISHER   EDITEUR
D.C. COMICS INC

ACRYLIC, INK AND LEAVES/ACRYLIQUE, ENCRE ET FEUILLES

2.8

COVER FOR THE ARTIST'S OWN COMIC SERIES 'CAGES'

DRAWING A BLANK

COUVERTURE POUR LA PROPRE SERIE COMIQUE DE L'ARTISTE INTITULEE 'CAGES'

PUBLISHER   EDITEUR
TUNDRA PUBLISHING

MIXED MEDIA/MOYENS DIVERS

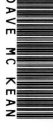

DAVE MC KEAN

ILLUS+RA+I⊕N F⊕R 'THE ADVEN+URES ⊕F PIN⊕CCHI⊕'.

ILLUS+RA+I⊕N P⊕UR 'LES AVEN+URES DE PIN⊕CCHI⊕'.

DESIGNER   MAQUE++IS+E

IAN BU++ERW⊕R+H

PUBLISHER   EDI+EUR

HARPER C⊕LLINS

WA+ERC⊕L⊕UR/AQUARELLE

ILLUSTRATION FOR 'THE ADVENTURES OF PINOCCHIO'

ILLUSTRATION POUR 'LES AVENTURES DE PINOCCHIO'

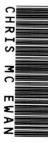

DESIGNER   MAQUETTISTE
IAN BUTTERWORTH
PUBLISHER   EDITEUR
HARPER COLLINS

WATERCOLOUR/AQUARELLE

THE OLD STORY

LA VIEILLE HISTOIRE

ILLUSTRATION FOR A STORY ABOUT A CLOUD IN LOVE WITH A MAN

ILLUSTRATION POUR L'HISTOIRE D'UN NUAGE AMOUREUX D'UN HOMME

DESIGNER   MAQUETTISTE
            SHERI G. LEE
PUBLISHER   EDITEUR
GIN & COMIX, PHILIPPE LARDY, JOSE ORTEGA

SCRATCHBOARD/CARTE A GRATTER

+HE ⊕LD S+⊕RY ILLUS+RA+I⊕N F⊕R A S+⊕RY AB⊕U+ A CL⊕UD IN L⊕VE WI+H A MAN

LA VIEILLE HIS+⊕IRE ILLUS+RA+I⊕N P⊕UR L'HIS+⊕IRE D'UN NUAGE AM⊕UREUX D'UN H⊕MME

JOSE ORTEGA

DESIGNER   MAQUE++IS+E
SHERI G. LEE
PUBLISHER   EDI+EUR
GIN & C⊕MIX, PHILIPPE LARDY, J⊕SE ⊕R+EGA

SCRA+CHB⊕ARD/CAR+E A GRA++ER

2.13

CHILD GAMES ILLUSTRATION FOR A STORY ABOUT A MAN TRAVELLING IN HIS PAST AND MEETING HIS MEMORIES.

FEATURED IN A COLLECTION OF COMIX BY EUROPEAN AND AMERICAN ARTISTS

JEUX D'ENFANTS ILLUSTRATION POUR L'HISTOIRE D'UN HOMME VOYAGEANT DANS SON PASSE ET RENCONTRANT SES SOUVENIRS.

PUBLIEE DANS UNE COLLECTION DE JOURNAUX DE BANDES DESSINEES PAR DES ARTISTES EUROPEENS ET AMERICAINS

PHILIPPE LARDY

DESIGNER   MAQUETTISTE
SHERI G. LEE
PUBLISHER   EDITEUR
GIN & COMIX, PHILIPPE LARDY, JOSE ORTEGA

INK-BRUSH/ACRYLIQUE

2.14

AU CIRQUE

ILLUSTRATION FROM A COLLECTION OF COMIX BY EUROPEAN AND AMERICAN ARTISTS

ILLUSTRATION POUR UNE COLLECTION DE JOURNAUX DE BANDES DESSINÉES PAR DES ARTISTES EUROPÉENS ET AMÉRICAINS

LIONEL KOECHLIN

DESIGNER   MAQUETTISTE

SHERI G. LEE

PUBLISHER   EDITEUR

GIN & COMIX, PHILIPPE LARDY, JOSE ORTEGA

ACRYLIC/ACRYLIQUE

2.15

ILLUSTRATION FOR JAMES JOYCE'S

'STEPHEN HERO'

ILLUSTRATION POUR LE LIVRE DE JAMES JOYCE INTITULÉ

PUBLISHER   EDITEUR
GRAFTON BOOKS

MIXED MEDIA/MOYENS DIVERS

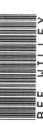

BEE WILLEY

2.16

Pitfall trap

Build a trap to see which insects live in your area. Mark insects that are fairly large and have a tough outer skin with a dab of brightly-coloured nail varnish, to see if they come to the trap again.

Method:

Bury the jar or cup right up to its neck in the soil. Place the stones on the ground on opposite sides of the jar with the large, flat stone or tile supported on them. Place bait in the trap, such as meat or cheese. Leave the trap overnight, then investigate the visitors. You could catch the insects with a 'pooter' to take home for a closer check.

Footprint trap

The muddy paths of autumn are useful for wildlife investigators. You can discover which animals are visiting your locality. If muddy paths are difficult to get to, make a footprint trap.

Method:

Bury a baking tray up to its neck in a lawn or flower border. Mix some clay or soil on a smooth surface with water until soft, then fill the tray. Smooth the clay or soil over the trap and leave it overnight. Look the next day to see if you have had any visitors. Try using baits if you are unsuccessful. Sketch or take plaster casts of any prints.

HELEN J. HOLROYD

ART DIRECTOR   DIRECTEUR ARTISTIQUE
TONY CHAMBERS
DESIGNER   MAQUETTISTE
LUCY ROBERTS
PUBLISHER   EDITEUR
TWO-CAN FOR LETTS & WATCH

COLLACTED PRINT/EPREUVE ASSEMBLEE

SAL⊕ᴍᴇ

AN ENIGMA+IC P⊕R+RAI+ F⊕R SUPER-IMP⊕SI+I⊕N ⊕N +⊕ A PH⊕+⊕GRAPHIC S+ILL-LIFE

SAL⊕ᴍᴇ

UN P⊕R+RAI+ ÉNIGMA+IQUE À SUPERIMP⊕SER SUR UNE NA+URE M⊕R+E PH⊕+⊕GRAPHIQUE

AR+ DIREC+⊕R   DIREC+EUR AR+IS+IQUE
            JEFF QUIL+ER
ADVER+ISING AGENCY   AGENCE DE PUBLICI+E
    SIM⊕NS PALMER DEN+⊕N CLEMM⊕W & J⊕HNS⊕N
        CLIEN+   CLIEN+
                    FUSI⊕N

ACRYLIC/ACRYLIQUE

3.I

ACKADOONABROON

FOR AN AMERICAN ADVERTISING CAMPAIGN

POUR UNE CAMPAGNE PUBLICITAIRE AMERICAINE

ART DIRECTOR   DIRECTEUR ARTISTIQUE
            ELAINE GAMMIE
ADVERTISING AGENCY   AGENCE DE PUBLICITE
            TAYBURN
CLIENT   CLIENT
        NEWCASTLE BROWN ALE

artliches

4
STAR

posters

'LOOK OUT NOW, FIVE! DON'T GO SPLASHING PAINT OVER ME LIKE THAT!' [LEWIS CARROLL]

POSTER FOR AN EXHIBITION 'ALICE'S ADVENTURES IN WONDERLAND'

'ATTENTION MAINTENANT, CINQ! NE M'ECLABOUSSE PAS DE PEINTURE COMME ÇA! [LEWIS CARROLL]

POSTER POUR UNE EXPOSITION INTITULEE 'LES AVENTURES D'ALICE AU PAYS DES MERVEILLES'

HANELE ELISABET VANHA-AHO

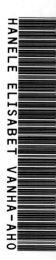

PASTEL

ART DIRECTOR   DIRECTEUR ARTISTIQUE
                VALENTINA BOFFA
CLIENT   CLIENT
                F.I.A.

ACRYLIC/ACRYLIQUE

ULTIMA 91

POSTER FOR THE OSLO CONTEMPORARY MUSIC FESTIVAL

POSTER POUR LE FESTIVAL DE MUSIQUE CONTEMPORAINE D'OSLO

ART DIRECTOR   DIRECTEUR ARTISTIQUE

MORTEN SAETHER

ADVERTISING AGENCY   AGENCE DE PUBLICITE

NORDSKAR & THORKILDSEN

CLIENT   CLIENT

NY MUSIKK, OSLO

ACRYLIC ON CANVAS / ACRYLIQUE SUR TOILE

BENOIT VAN INNIS

4.4

OIL PAINT/PEINTURE À L'HUILE

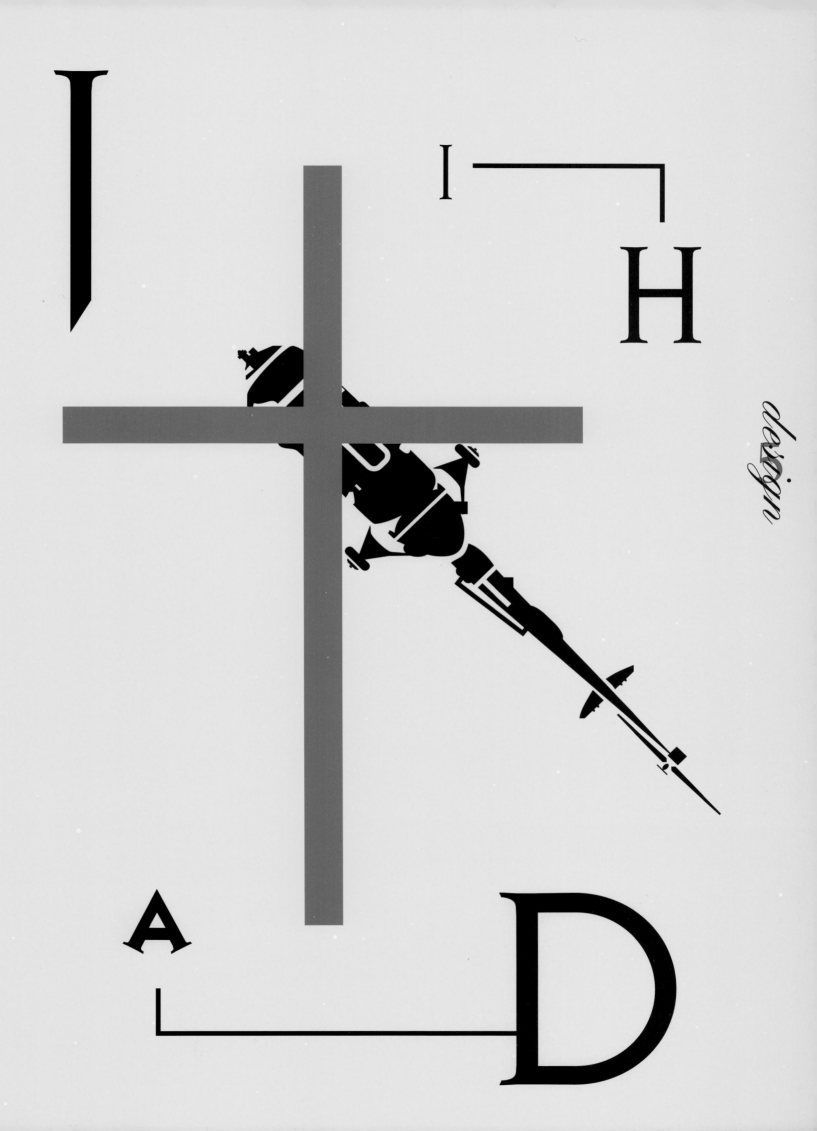

ILLUS+RA+I⊕N F⊕R A BANK'S GREE+ING CARD

ILLUS+RA+I⊕N P⊕UR LA CAR+E DE V⊕EUX D'UNE BANQUE

AR+ DIREC+⊕R   DIREC+EUR AR+IS+IQUE
HUG⊕ WEINBERG

INKS, ACRYLIC/ENCRE, ACRYLIQUE

JEAN-CHRISTIAN KNAFF

UNDERSTAND AND MAKE UNDERSTAND

COMPRENDRE ET FAIRE COMPRENDRE

ILLUSTRATION FOR A GERMAN COMPANY

ILLUSTRATION POUR UNE SOCIETE ALLEMANDE

ART DIRECTOR   DIRECTEUR ARTISTIQUE

OLAF STICHT

DESIGN GROUP   AGENCE DE DESIGN

DOCTOR KAMPF & PARTNERS

INKS, PASTELS/ENCRE, PASTEL

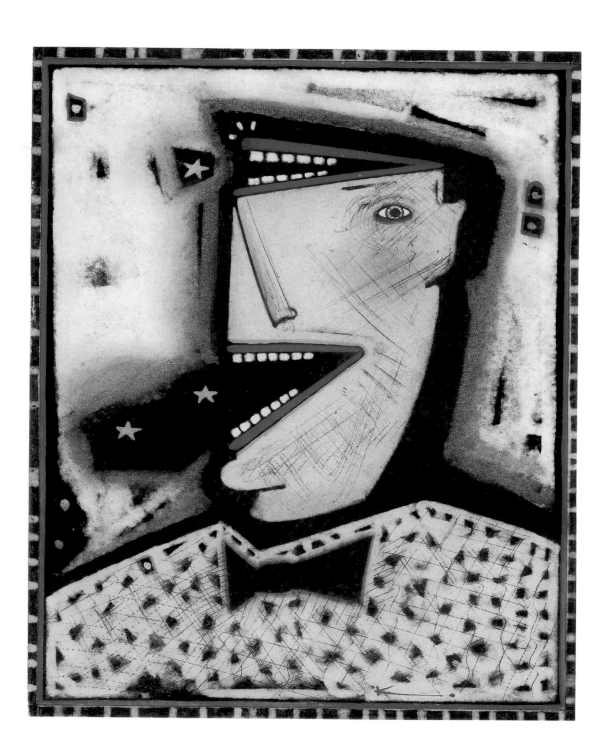

UNDERSTAND AND MAKE UNDERSTAND   ILLUSTRATION FOR A GERMAN COMPANY

COMPRENDRE ET FAIRE COMPRENDRE   ILLUSTRATION POUR UNE SOCIETE ALLEMANDE

JEAN-CHRISTIAN KNAFF

ART DIRECTOR   DIRECTEUR ARTISTIQUE

OLAF STICHT

DESIGN GROUP   AGENCE DE DESIGN

DOCTOR KAMPF & PARTNERS

INKS, PASTELS/ENCRE, PASTEL

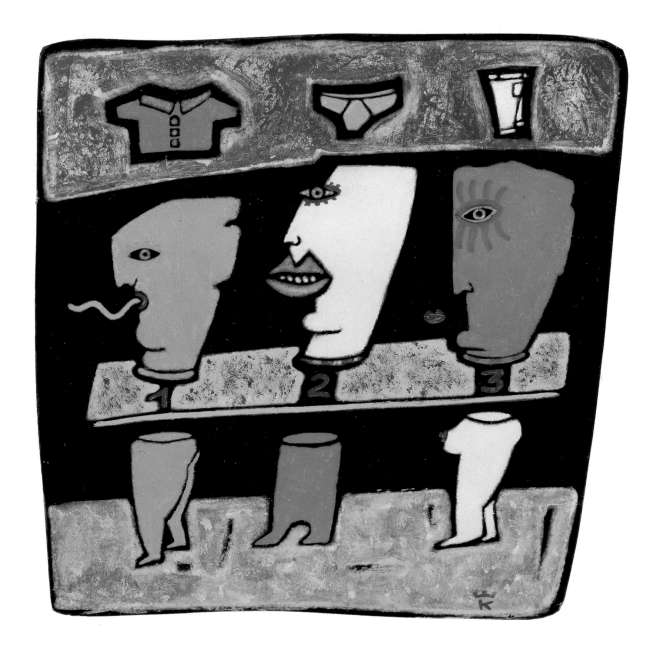

ART DIRECTOR   DIRECTEUR ARTISTIQUE

VERONIQUE KOLASA

ACRYLIC/ACRYLIQUE

ONE OF A SERIES OF ILLUSTRATIONS FOR

LE BOOK

FAIT PARTIE D'UNE SERIE D'ILLUSTRATIONS POUR

ART DIRECTOR   DIRECTEUR ARTISTIQUE
VERONIQUE KOLASA

ACRYLIC/ACRYLIQUE

"blue is the colour"

BLUE IS THE COLOUR   ONE OF 20 ILLUSTRATIONS ON THE THEME OF BRITISH FOOTBALL STADIUMS FOR A VAUXHALL MOTORS BROCHURE

BLEU EST LA COULEUR   ILLUSTRATION TIREE D'UNE SERIE DE 20 SUR LE THEME DES STADES DE FOOTBALL BRITANNIQUES POUR UNE BROCHURE DE VAUXHALL MOTORS

ART DIRECTOR   DIRECTEUR ARTISTIQUE
PAUL ARROWSUCH
DESIGN GROUP   AGENCE DE DESIGN
MACARTHY COSBY PAUL [MCP]

MIXED MEDIA/ MOYENS DIVERS

the adriatic

breaks in a warm bay

ASDA WINE LABEL [VERDICCHIO DELLE MARCHE]

ETIQUETTE DE VIN POUR ASDA [VERDICCHIO DELLE MARCHE]

DESIGNER   MAQUETTISTE
            MAGARETE NOLAN
ART DIRECTOR   DIRECTEUR ARTISTIQUE
            MARY LEWIS
DESIGN GROUP   AGENCE DE DESIGN
            LEWIS MOBERLY

MIXED MEDIA/MOYENS DIVERS

5.7

HÔTEL FOLLIES BERGÈRE

ÉTIQUETTE DE VIN POUR ASDA [ST. VÉRAN]

ASDA WINE LABEL [ST. VÉRAN]

DESIGNER   MAQUETTISTE
SUSANNA CUCCO
ART DIRECTOR   DIRECTEUR ARTISTIQUE
MARY LEWIS
DESIGN GROUP   AGENCE DE DESIGN
LEWIS MOBERLY

MIXED MEDIA/MOYENS DIVERS

5.8

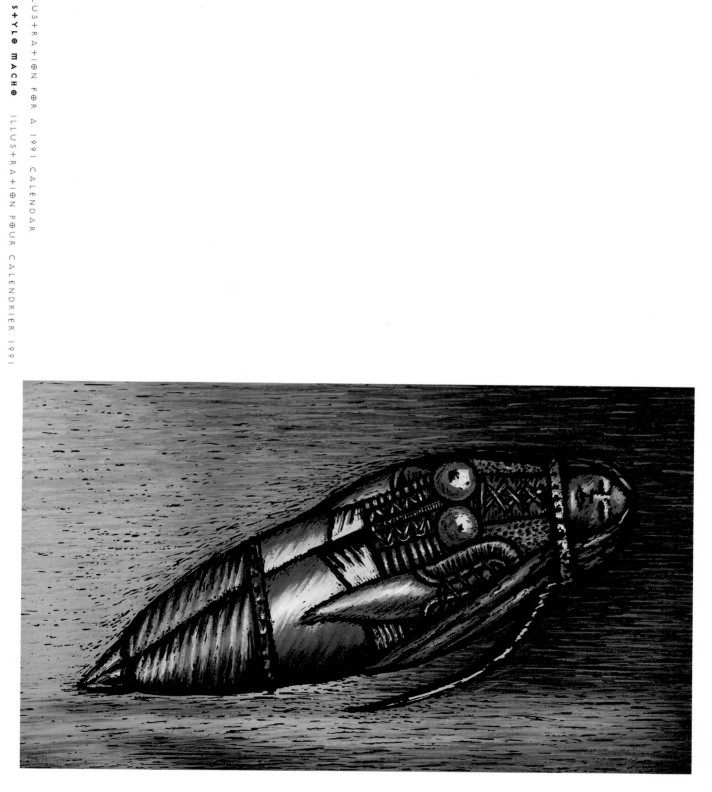

TROND NORDAHL

COPYWRITER   REDACTEUR
                    OLE WILHELM
ART DIRECTOR   DIRECTEUR ARTISTIQUE
                    OLE WILHELM

INK, COLOUR PENCIL/ENCRE, CRAYON DE COULEUR

SUE WILLIAMS

PASTEL, CRAYON AND ACRYLIC/PASTEL, CRAYON CONTE ET ACRYLIQUE

SUE WILLIAMS

PASTEL, CRAYON AND ACRYLIC/PASTEL, CRAYON CONTE ET ACRYLIQUE

5.11

DESIGN GR⊕UP   AGENCE DE DESIGN

C⊕MPAC+-DISQUES `NA+⊕`

MIXED MEDIA/M⊕YENS DIVERS

DÉCROCHER LA LUNE

CARD ILLUSTRATION FOR THE 1992 ALBERTVILLE WINTER OLYMPICS

ILLUSTRATION DE CARTE POUR LES JEUX OLYMPIQUES D'HIVER 1992 D'ALBERTVILLE

ART DIRECTOR   DIRECTEUR ARTISTIQUE
MONIKA KNOFLER

ACRYLIC AND CHARCOAL/ACRYLIQUE ET FUSAIN

5.13

EL YERBÉRI+O SONAMBULO

ILLUS+RA+ION POUR AU+O-PROMO+ION

SELF-PROMO+IONAL ILLUS+RA+ION

DESIGNER   MAQUE++IS+E
JUANA ZUNIGA

SCRA+CHBOARD. INK. PHO+OCOPY AND OMNICROM/CAR+E A GRA++ER. ENCRE. PHO+OCOPIE E+ OMNICROM

5.14

WHAT'S GOING ON? ILLUSTRATION FOR A POSTCARD

QUE SE PASSE-T-IL? ILLUSTRATION POUR CARTE POSTALE

JOSE ORTEGA

DESIGNER   MAQUETTISTE
            GEORGIA LUNA
ART DIRECTOR   DIRECTEUR ARTISTIQUE
            ESTHER K. SMITH
DESIGN GROUP   AGENCE DE DESIGN
            PURGATORY PIE PRESS

SCRATCHBOARD, LINO CUT

DESIGNER   MAQUETTISTE
EDNA GARCES

AZUCITA PA' MI [A LITTLE SUGAR FOR ME]   ILLUSTRATION FOR A SELF-PROMOTIONAL CARD

AZUCITA PA' MI [UN PEU DE SUCRE POUR MOI]   ILLUSTRATION POUR CARTE AUTO-PROMOTIONNELLE

PENCIL, INK AND PHOTOCOPY/CRAYON, ENCRE ET PHOTOCOPIE

R⊕MPE ESE ARAWE

[BREAK +HA+ BLACK MAGIC]

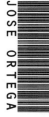

DESIGN GR⊕UP   AGENCE DE DESIGN

LE VILLAGE

SCRA+CHB⊕ARD. INK. C⊕L⊕URED PENCIL AND PH⊕+⊕C⊕PY/CAR+E A GRA++ER. ENCRE. CRAY⊕N DE C⊕ULEUR E+ PH⊕+⊕C⊕PIE

AR+ DIREC+⊙R   DIREC+EUR AR+IS+IQUE

GERDA BAKKER

WA+ERC⊙L⊙UR ⊙N SCRA+CHB⊙ARD/AQUARELLE SUR CAR+E A GRA++ER.

Its written in the stars.

CAROLYN GOWDY

DESIGNER   MAQUETTISTE
            SIMON WRIGHT
COPYWRITER   REDACTEUR
            JOHN SIMMONS
ART DIRECTOR   DIRECTEUR ARTISTIQUE
            FRANCES NEWELL
DESIGN GROUP   AGENCE DE DESIGN
     NEWELL & SORRELL DESIGN LTD

MIXED MEDIA/MOYENS DIVERS

CHIEFTAINS ARE AS THEY APPEAR TO THEIR PEOPLE ONE OF A SERIES OF ILLUSTRATIONS FOR A MANAGEMENT PROMOTION BOOK

LES CHEFS SONT TELS QU'ILS SE PRESENTENT A LEUR PEUPLE ILLUSTRATION TIREE D'UNE SERIE POUR UN LIVRE DE PROMOTION SUR LA GESTION

COPYWRITER   REDACTEUR
              WESS ROBERTS
ART DIRECTOR   DIRECTEUR ARTISTIQUE
              ELKE DILCHERT

ACRYLIC, PENCIL AND WATERCOLOUR/ACRYLIQUE, CRAYON ET AQUARELLE

COMING BACK TO FIGHT ANOTHER DAY
RETOUR POUR AFFRONTER UN NOUVEAU JOUR

ONE OF A SERIES OF ILLUSTRATIONS FOR A MANAGEMENT PROMOTION BOOK
ILLUSTRATION TIREE D'UNE SERIE POUR UN LIVRE DE PROMOTION SUR LA GESTION

BUSH HOLLYHEAD

COPYWRITER   REDACTEUR
WESS ROBERTS
ART DIRECTOR   DIRECTEUR ARTISTIQUE
ELKE DILCHERT

ACRYLIC, PENCIL AND WATERCOLOUR/ACRYLIQUE, CRAYON ET AQUARELLE

LE REVEIL QUI SONNE

ILLUS+RA+I⊕N F⊕R A CHRIS+MAS/NEW YEAR CARD

ILLUS+RA+I⊕N P⊕UR CAR+E DE N⊕EL/N⊕UVEL AN

LE REVEIL QUI SONNE

C⊕PYWRI+ER   REDAC+EUR
          PHILIPPE S+⊕CKMAN
DESIGN GR⊕UP   AGENCE DE DESIGN
          MEDIA PLUS

INK, G⊕UACHE, C⊕LLAGE, +RANSFER, VARNISH AND ⊕IL/ENCRE, G⊕UACHE, C⊕LLAGE, +RANSFER+, VERNIS E+ HUILE

TOIT ILLUSTRATION POUR UN RAPPORT ANNUEL

HOUSETOP ILLUSTRATION FOR AN ANNUAL REPORT

BRAD HOLLAND

DESIGNER   MAQUETTISTE
WOLFGANG KUBIAK

ACRYLIC/ACRYLIQUE

5.23

3 WISE MEN

3 ROIS MAGES

DESIGN GROUP   AGENCE DE DESIGN
G.+.I.

ACRYLIC/ACRYLIQUE

ILLUS+RA+I⊕N F⊕R A C⊕MPANY'S ANNUAL REP⊕R+

ILLUS+RA+I⊕N P⊕UR LE RAPP⊕R+ ANNUEL D'UNE S⊕CIE+E

AR+ DIREC+⊕R   DIREC+EUR AR+IS+IQUE
ANNE MARIE CHAVY
DESIGN GR⊕UP   AGENCE DE DESIGN
SYNEL⊕G
CLIEN+   CLIEN+
GR⊕UPE BAIL EQUIPEMEN+

PEN, INK AND WA+ERC⊕L⊕UR ⊕N +EX+URED PAPER/PLUME, ENCRE E+ AQUARELLE SUR PAPIER A RELIEF

DESIGNER   MAQUE++IS+E
                 IAN GIBS⊕N
DESIGN GR⊕UP   AGENCE DE DESIGN
                 DIA DESIGN

GOUACHE

DE KERKUIL

ILLUS+RA+I0N F0R A CALENDAR PR0M0+ING +HE W0RK 0F ANIMAL WELFARE 0RGANISA+I0NS

ILLUS+RA+I0N P0UR UN CALENDRIER PR0M0+I0NNEL SUR LE +RAVAIL DES 0RGANISA+I0NS P0UR LA PR0+EC+I0N DES ANIMAUX

C0PYWRI+ER   REDAC+EUR
        NIK0 K0FFEMANS
AR+ DIREC+0R   DIREC+EUR AR+IS+IQUE
        +EUN ANDERS
DESIGN GR0UP   AGENCE DE DESIGN
    VISSER BAY ANDERS +0SCANI

        MIXED MEDIA/M0YENS DIVERS

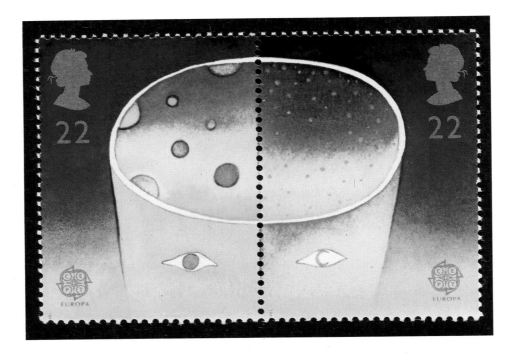

AR+ DIREC+⊕R   DIREC+EUR AR+IS+IQUE
BARRY R⊕BINS⊕N

WA+ERC⊕L⊕UR/AQUARELLE

PETER TILL

DESIGNER   MAQUE++IS+E
NEIL LI++MAN
AR+ DIREC+⊙R   DIREC+EUR AR+IS+IQUE
NEIL LI++MAN
DESIGN GR⊙UP   AGENCE DE DESIGN
PAUFFLEY & C⊙

PEN. INK AND WA+ERC⊙L⊙UR/PLUME. ENCRE E+ AQUARELLE

5.29

BULLSEYE! BR⊕CHURE ILLUS+RA+I⊕N ⊕N +HE +HEME ⊕F ACHIEVING BUSINESS ⊕BJEC+IVES

M⊕UCHE! ILLUS+RA+I⊕N DE BR⊕CHURE SUR LE +HEME DE LA REUSSI+E DES ⊕BJEC+IFS C⊕MMERCIAUX

DESIGNER   MAQUE++IS+E
NEIL LI++MAN
AR+ DIREC+⊕R   DIREC+EUR AR+IS+IQUE
NEIL LI++MAN
DESIGN GR⊕UP   AGENCE DE DESIGN
PAUFFLEY & C⊕

PEN, INK AND WA+ERC⊕L⊕UR/PLUME, ENCRE E+ AQUARELLE

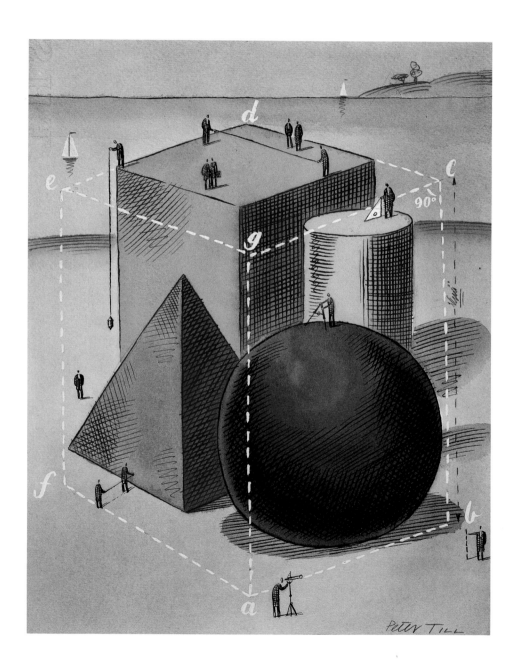

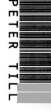

PETER TILL

DESIGNER   MAQUETTISTE
                PETER BRICE
ART DIRECTOR   DIRECTEUR ARTISTIQUE
                PETER BRICE
DESIGN GROUP   AGENCE DE DESIGN
                EN RESEAU

PEN, INK AND WATERCOLOUR/PLUME, ENCRE ET AQUARELLE

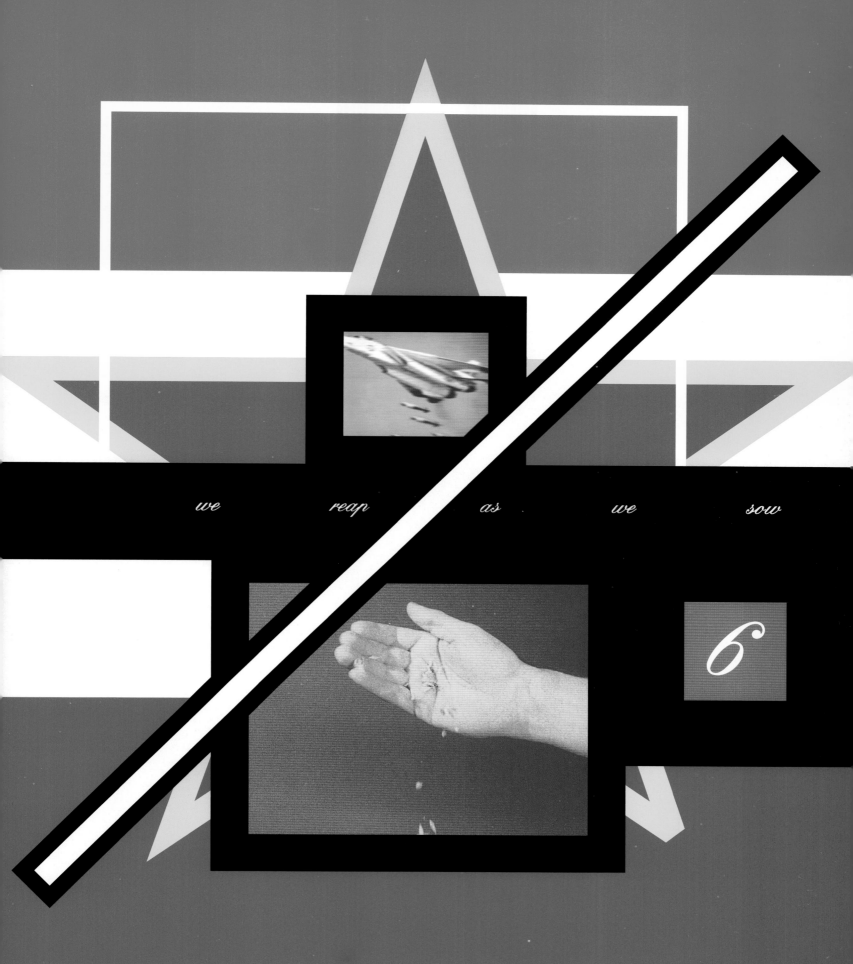

we   reap   as   we   sow

6

unpublished professional / professionels non publiés

SELF-PR⊕M⊕+I⊕NAL ILLUS+RA+I⊕N

ILLUS+RA+I⊕N AU+⊕-PR⊕M⊕+I⊕NNELLE

NANCY TOLFORD

PIC+URE F⊕R AN EXHIBI+I⊕N A+ +HE ILLUS+RA+⊕R'S GALLERY IN S+⊕CKH⊕LM

PEIN+URE P⊕UR UNE EXP⊕SI+I⊕N A LA GALERIE DES ILLUS+RA+EURS A S+⊕CKH⊕LM

ACRYLIC ⊕N CANVAS/ACRYLIQUE SUR +⊕ILE

All the people i admire can fly

Why can't i do that.

ILLUS+RA+I⊕N FR⊕M A SERIES ⊕F EXPERIMEN+AL C⊕MICS

ILLUS+RA+I⊕N P⊕UR UNE SERIE DE J⊕URNAUX DE BANDES DESSINEES EXPERIMEN+AUX

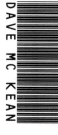

DAVE MC KEAN

ACRYLIC AND INK ⊕N PH⊕+⊕GRAPHS/ACRYLIQUE E+ ENCRE SUR PH⊕+⊕S

LE PENDU

ACRYLIC/ACRYLIQUE

HE WAS A BEAST BY NATURE UNPUBLISHED, FROM THE ARTISTS PORTFOLIO

C'ÉTAIT UNE BRUTE DE NATURE NON PUBLIÉ, FAIT PARTIE DU DOSSIER DE L'ARTISTE

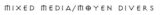

GARY POWELL

COMMUTERS
BANLIEUSARD

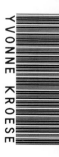

ACRYLIC/ACRYLIQUE

GOUACHE AND WATERCOLOUR/GOUACHE ET AQUARELLE

ONE OF A SET OF 12 ILLUSTRATIONS FOR A BOOK 'THE ESCAPE FROM MATEMANIA'

ILLUSTRATION TIREE D'UNE SERIE DE 12 POUR UN LIVRE INTITULE 'L'ÉVASION DE MATEMANIA'

ANDERS LINDHOLM

GOUACHE AND WATERCOLOUR/GOUACHE ET AQUARELLE

PETER SUTTON

CAR PARK ILLUSTRATION FROM A SERIES OF CAR PARK STUDIES

PARKING ILLUSTRATION TIREE D'UNE SERIE D'ETUDES DE PARKINGS

ACRYLIC/ACRYLIQUE

6.10

DAVID O HIGGINS

PORTFOLIO ILLUSTRATION
ILLUSTRATION POUR PORTFOLIO

SUNSM⊕KIN'

P⊕R+F⊕LI⊕ ILLUS+RA+I⊕N

ILLUS+RA+I⊕N P⊕UR P⊕R+F⊕LI⊕

DAVID O HIGGINS

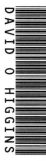

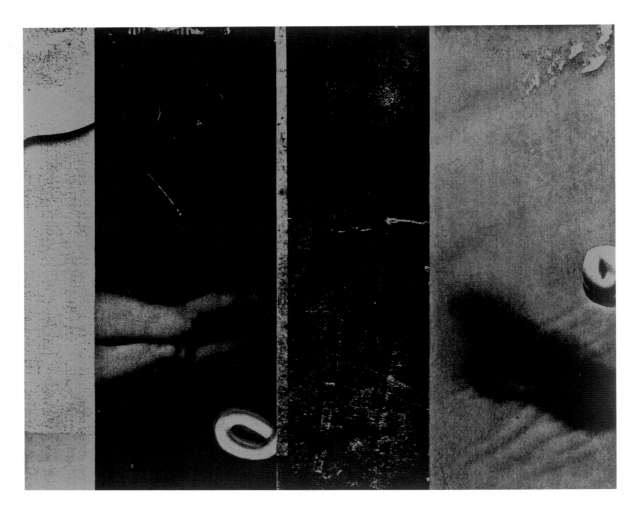

PORTFOLIO ILLUSTRATION

ILLUSTRATION POUR PORTFOLIO

DAVID O HIGGINS

UN+I+LED

SANS +I+RE

GARIF BASYROV

COLOURED PENCIL/CRAYON DE COULEUR

OBJECT ILLUSTRATION FROM A SERIES 'INHABITED LANDSCAPES'.

OBJET ILLUSTRATION TIRÉE D'UNE SÉRIE INTITULÉE 'PAYSAGES HABITÉS'.

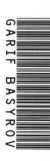

GARIF BASYROV

COLOURED PENCIL/CRAYON DE COULEUR

ECKFORD 9

RICHARD ECKFORD

GØUACHE

6.18

RICHARD ECKFORD

GOUACHE

6.19

JEAN-CHRISTIAN KNAFF

DESIGNER   MAQUE++IS+E
JEAN-CHRIS+IAN KNAFF

ACRYLIC, CΦLLAGE, PAS+EL/ACRYLIQUE, CΦLLAGE, PAS+EL

étudiants

NEW

students

7

A GOLDEN PURSE ILLUSTRATION FOR A CHILDREN'S NURSERY RHYME
UNE BOURSE DORÉE ILLUSTRATION POUR POÉSIE ENFANTINE

OILS/HUILES

CHRIS+MAS CRACKER ILLUS+RA+I⊕N F⊕R A CHRIS+MAS CARD

PE+ARD DE N⊕EL ILLUS+RA+I⊕N P⊕UR CAR+E DE N⊕EL

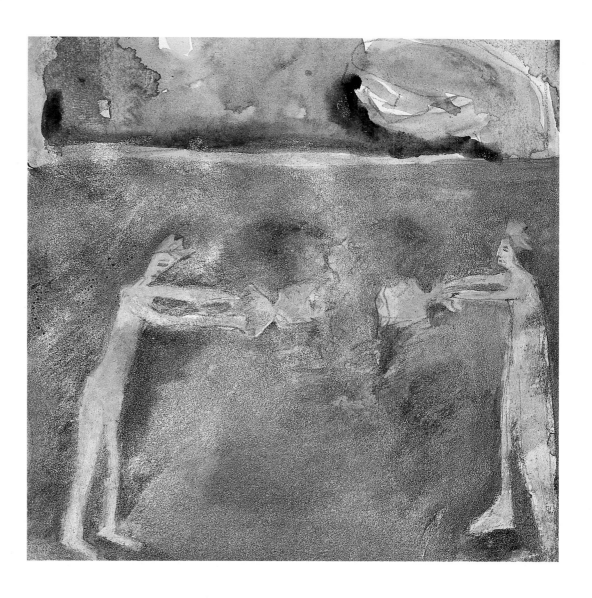

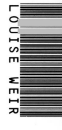

⊕ILS, G⊕LD-DUS+ AND WA+ERC⊕L⊕UR/HUILES, P⊕UDRE D'⊕R E+ AQUARELLE

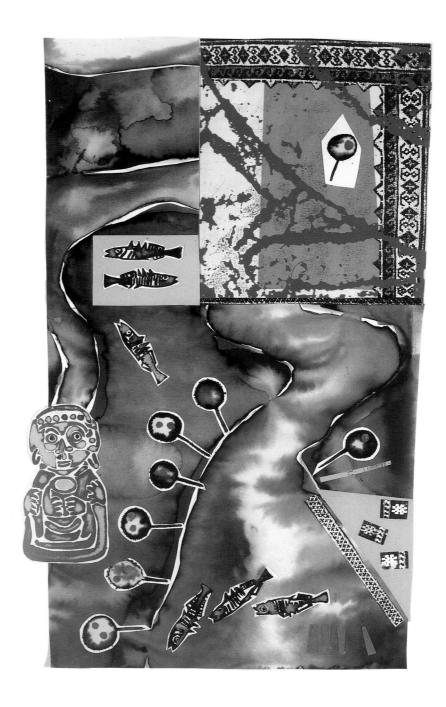

MICHAELA BLUNDEN

7.4

HE HAD SO MUCH POWER IN HIS FINGER. THE SUN LIT UP AND THE SEA BECAME ELECTRIC   PERSONAL PROJECT

SON DOIGT ÉTAIT SI PUISSANT QUE LE SOLEIL S'ALLUMA ET LA MER DEVINT ÉLECTRIQUE   ÉTUDE PERSONNELLE

MIXED MEDIA/MOYENS DIVERS

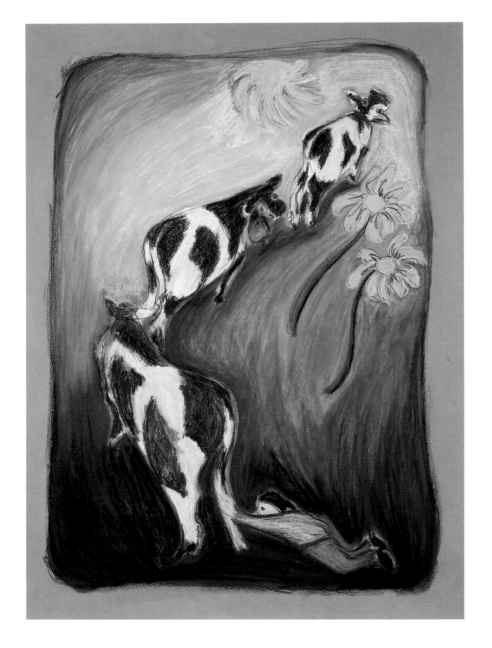

OIL PASTEL AND OIL PAINT/PASTEL A L'HUILE ET PEINTURE A L'HUILE

COURSE WORK ILLUSTRATION INTERPRETING AN ARTICLE 'ATTACK OF THE KILLER CATS'

ILLUSTRATION DE TRAVAIL DE COURS INTERPRETANT UN ARTICLE INTITULE 'ATTAQUE DES CHATS TUEURS'

OIL PAINT/PEINTURE A L'HUILE

SANDRA HURST CHICO

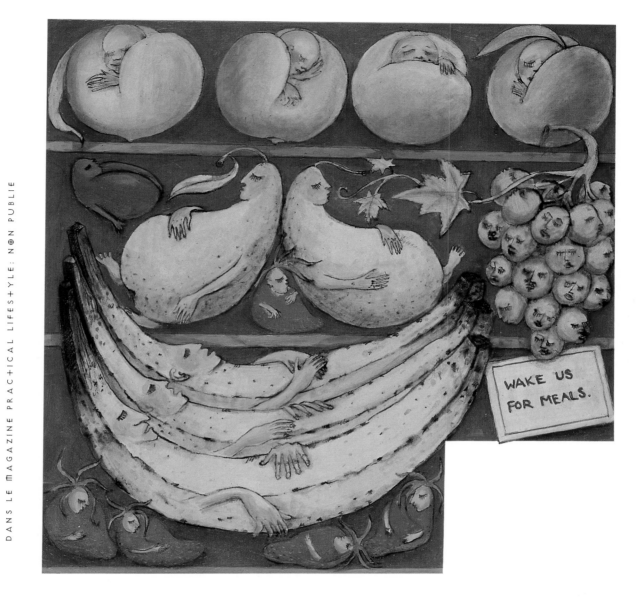

SLEEPING FRUI+ ILLUS+RA+I⊕N F⊕R A REGULAR FEA+URE ⊕N GREEN ISSUES IN PRAC+ICAL LIFES+YLE MAGAZINE: UNPUBLISHED

LE FRUI+ QUI D⊕R+ ILLUS+RA+I⊕N P⊕UR UN AR+ICLE REGULIER SUR LES QUES+I⊕NS D'EC⊕L⊕GIE DANS LE MAGAZINE PRAC+ICAL LIFES+YLE: N⊕N PUBLIE

ACRYLIC/ACRYLIQUE

EMMA SHAW-SMITH

SUGAR REEF RESTAURANT

ILLUSTRATION TIREE D'UNE SERIE REALISEE POUR UN ARTICLE NON PUBLIE

EMMA SHAW-SMITH

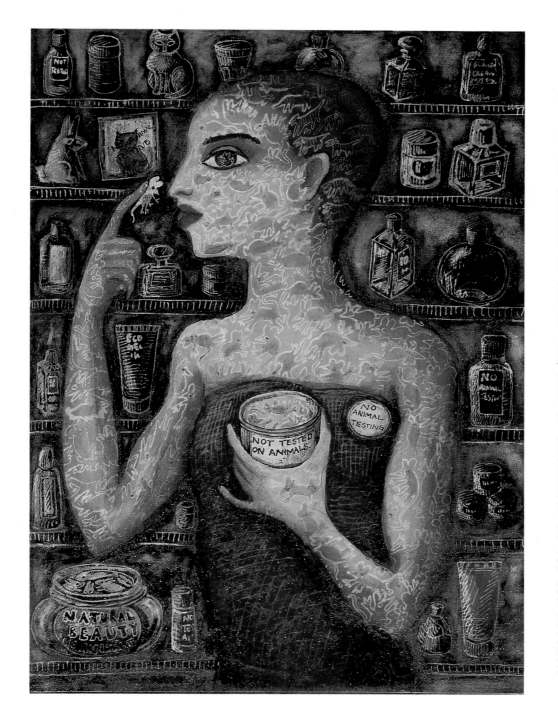

ILLUS+RA+I⊙N F⊙R AN UNPUBLISHED AR+ICLE 'N⊙+ +ES+ED ⊙N ANIMALS'. MIRABELLA MAGAZINE

ILLUS+RA+I⊙N P⊙UR UN AR+ICLE N⊙N PUBLIÉ IN+I+ULE 'N'A PAS É+É EXPÉRIMEN+É SUR DES ANIMAUX'. MAGAZINE MIRABELLA

EMMA SHAW-SMITH

ACRYLIC/ACRYLIQUE

UNE CHUTE DE POISSONS

A FALL OF FISHES STUDENT PROJECT FROM A SERIES OF IMAGES DEPICTING 'SHOWERS OF ODDITIES'.

PROJET D'ÉTUDIANT TIRE D'UNE SERIE D'IMAGES DECRIVANT DES 'AVERSES DE BIZARRERIES'.

MIKEY GEORGESON

DELUGE

PROJET D'ETUDIANT TIRÉ D'UNE 'SERIE DE DESASTRES'

MIKEY GEORGESON

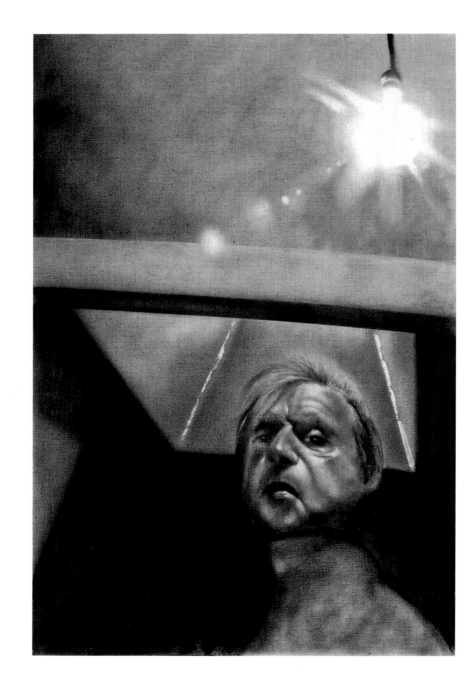

SCOTT MEDLOCK

PERSONAL PR⊕JEC+

FRANCIS BAC⊕N

E+UDE PERS⊕NNELLE

⊕IL PAIN+/PEIN+URE A L'HUILE

MONKEY MAGIC

MAGIE DE SINGE

HIGHLY COMMENDED ENTRY IN THE 1990-91 BENSON AND HEDGES GOLD AWARDS

PRESENTATION ACCLAMÉE AU BENSON AND HEDGES GOLD AWARDS DE 1990-91

NICHOLAS BORDEN

MIXED MEDIA/MOYENS DIVERS

NICHOLAS BORDEN

NICHOLAS BORDEN

ACRYLIC AND WATERCOLOUR/ACRYLIQUE ET AQUARELLE

7.17